A Williamson *Read-&-Do* Book

EASY ART FUN!

Do-it-yourself crafts for beginning readers

Jill Frankel Hauser

Illustrations by Savlan Hauser

WILLIAMSON PUBLISHING CHARLOTTE, VERMONT

Library of Congress Cataloging-in-Publication Data

Hauser, Jill Frankel, 1950-
   Easy art fun! : do-it-yourself crafts for beginning readers / Jill Frankel Hauser.
     p. cm. – (A Little Hands read-&-do book)
   Includes index.
   Contents: Colors are cool! -- Snappy snips -- Let's play! -- For you and me -- Let's pretend -- Colorful music -- Wearable art.
   Summary: A collection of instructions for craft projects that can be read and followed by beginning readers.
   ISBN 1-885593-62-7 (pbk.)
   1. Early childhood education--Activity programs--Juvenile literature. 2. Reading (Early childhood)--Juvenile literature. 3. Handicraft--Juvenile literature. [1. Reading. 2. Handicraft.] I. Title. II. Series.

LB1139.35.A37 H38 2002
372.5--dc21
                                        2002026820

Little Hands® series editor: **Susan Williamson**
Project editor: **Dana Pierson**
Interior design: **Marie Ferrante-Doyle**
Illustrations: **Savlan Hauser**
Cover design: **Monkey Barrel Design**
Cover photos: **David A. Seaver**
Printing: **Capital City Press**

Williamson Publishing Co.
P.O. Box 185 • Charlotte, VT 05445
(800) 234-8791

Manufactured in the United States of America

10 9 8 7 6 5 4 3 2

Dedication

To Mary Hauser, to whom art is both a beacon and a way of life.

Acknowledgments

Thank you to my Rother kindergartners. Your passion to create revealed that the wellspring of art lies within us all, ready to be tapped.

Contents

To Kid Artists

Yes, you can be an artist!

You can cut.
You can paste.
You can draw.
You can paint.

This book is filled with art ideas to try. Would you like to make a Pet Dino? What about a Wake-Up Puppet? Or a Fast Frame? All the steps are right here, just for you. Try the ideas for putting your own special touch on each project, too. That's the art part!

Yes! You can be a reader!

There is something special about this book. You can read it yourself (or with help from someone else).

You can read the pictures. Or, you can use the pictures to help you read the words. Soon you will be reading words on your own.
Here's how:

1. Read **Get it!** Read **Make it!**
2. Re-read **Get it!** as you gather supplies.
3. Re-read **Make it!** as you do the steps.

Wow! You just made cool art by yourself!

It's easy to read. It's easy to make. It's *Easy Art Fun!*

Art Words to Know

Get it! *It's easy to find these things around your house.*

 Colored paper

 Crayons

 Hole punch

 Index cards

 Magazines

 Markers

 Newspaper

 Paintbrushes

 Paper

 Paper bags

 Paper clips

 Paste, glue, or glue stick

 Scissors

 Stapler

 String

 Tape

 Tempera paints

 Watercolor paints

 Yarn

Art Words to Do

Make it! *It's fun to do art.*

Crumple
Curl
Decorate
Fill
Fold
Hang
Knot
Mix
Paint
Punch
Snip
Staple
Tear
Thread
Tie
Toss
Trace

Cut

Draw

Paste

To Grown-Ups

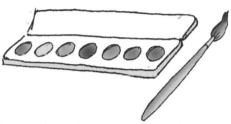

Empowering young artists

The art table in my kindergarten classroom has long been the most popular place to be during "choice time." It's the production site for the most marvelous creations: headgear with raggedy manes, carefully decorated boxes to hold precious treasures, endearing greeting cards for friends (and me, if I'm lucky), and humorous puppet characters from our favorite tales. With creativity already alive and well in my students, I've wondered how I can possibly teach these young artists anything.

So what can adults contribute? I have discovered that creativity soars if the artistic process involves the following:

- **An introduction of techniques** that children can readily apply to projects of their own design.

- **Opportunities for children** to move beyond the model to their own visions of the crafts.

- **Projects within the control of children**, requiring little or no adult help.

I know my teaching is on track when I hear, "Look, Mrs. Hauser. Remember the streamers we pasted onto our Flutter Fliers? That's how I made my puppet's hair!" Or, "I made a stuffed truck instead of a stuffed dinosaur." Or, even just the simple, "Look, I made it myself!"

Easy Art Fun! is the result of years of creating with children. Embedded in the activities are the key elements mentioned here. Open-ended projects teach art and craft techniques that can be applied to other original creations. "Yes, the spring mechanism in the Happy Pop-Up Card can add movement to any picture!" *More Fun!* sections challenge children to go beyond the model. Adult help is minimized to ensure that children are creators, not spectators.

These projects inspire children to think creatively and produce artistic masterpieces all on their own. Otherwise, how could the same wonder wand have worked magic for a whole group of diverse and imaginative young artists, all with their own special dreams?

Empowering young readers

Literacy is center stage in 21st-century classrooms, and rightfully so. The ability to read and write is widely recognized as key to a successful life. It is expected that children will learn to read in the primary grades so they can read to learn in grades three and above.

How can we make literacy appealing to young learners? Given that children are naturally drawn to making and doing, *art is the perfect door to literacy*. What better motivation to read than achieving an outcome that's meaningful to a child? So, flip through the pages of this book with your children and select a craft together. "Wow, this looks like fun. How do we make it? Let's *read* and find out!"

Modeling for pre-readers

For children who cannot yet read, you can help build *print awareness*. Model how to *read and do* by thinking aloud through the process:

> "First, I'll figure out what materials we need. Oh, here they are, listed under **Get it!**"

Point to the text as you read:

> "Paper, paste, markers, scissors. Now I need to plan the steps. They're here under **Make it!**"

Show how the pictures work with the text as you read the steps. Now, re-read as you gather materials and follow the steps. *Model* how important it is to refer back to the words and pictures to know just what to do. Continue to *point out features* that make each page so helpful:

> "These big, bold pictures help me know what to do. See how the steps are numbered? We need to do them in this order."

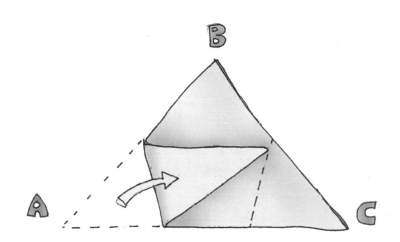

Guiding for beginners

For children who are just starting to read, point out how the pictures provide support for the words as you follow the techniques. Encourage children to join in the reading by sounding out or saying words they know while you read the rest. Continually refer to the text as the means to successful completion of the project.

Stepping back

If children can read, advise them to read all directions first, and then re-read as they work through the project. Now step back. Let them get materials and complete the steps by themselves, relying on the print, not on a grown-up, for support. Praise the project: "It's wonderful! And you did it on your own by reading the instructions!"

The message to the child is clear: Reading helped her have fun and make something she's proud of!

Teacher tips

• Copy each spread that contains a project onto 11" x 17" (27.5 x 42.5 cm) paper. Tape it to the wall. Use the photocopy like a "big book" to model reading as the means to the creation of the project.

• After children learn to make the project confidently, encourage them to make it again in their own way. Display the "big book" photocopy in your art center for an independent activity.

• To be sure your classroom offers a variety of reading opportunities to match diverse student interests, make *Easy Art Fun!* and other relevant, educational activity books part of your library. Whether for jobs, recreation, or using new technology, students must be able to negotiate the how-to text of manuals and instruction guides for success in the real world.

Colors Are Cool!

I Love to Color!

I love to color.

Yes, I do.

Red and yellow,

Green and blue.

With markers, paint,

And crayons, too.

I love to color!

(To the tune of "London Bridge Is Falling Down")

Super Scribble

Music can help you make nice colors and shapes!

Get it!

 Music

 Marker

 Paper

 Crayons

Make it!

1. Listen to music you like.

2. Hold a marker. Draw a big, loopy scribble to the music.

3. Use crayons to color in each small shape you made. Press hard for deep colors. Press gently for light colors.

What nice colors and shapes!

More Fun!

Make a dangle!
1. Cut out the super scribble.
2. Punch a hole near the top.
3. Hang from a string.

- Try all kinds of music.
- Try all kinds of shapes.

My Pet Dino

Dinosaurs lived long ago,
but you can play with one today!

Get it!

 Child safety scissors

 2 sheets of paper

 Tempera paint

red blue

 Paintbrush

 Stapler

 Old newspaper

Make it!

1. Cut out two dino shapes at the same time.

2. Paint the dinos. Let them dry.

3. Hold the two dinos together.
Staple along the edge.
Keep a spot open.

4. Crumple newspaper.
Fill the dino.
Staple the puffy dino shut.

Hello, pet dino!

More Fun!

Make it swish.
1. Tie string to the top.
2. Paste strips below.
3. Hang it up.

Any shape will work.
- Make a fish.
- Make the sun.
- Make a happy face.

Butterfly Buddy

Paint two pretty wings at the same time. They look alike!

Get it!

 White paper

 Tempera paint

 Paintbrush

 Child safety scissors

 Colored paper

 Pencil

 Paste

 Marker

Make it!

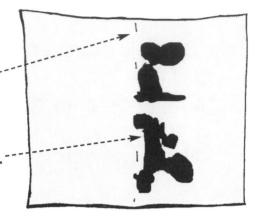

1. Fold the white paper in half.
   Open it up.

2. Drip paint blobs near the fold.

3. Re-fold the paper.
   Rub your hand on the fold.
   Push the paint up and down.

4. Open the paper.
   Let it dry.
   What does it look like?

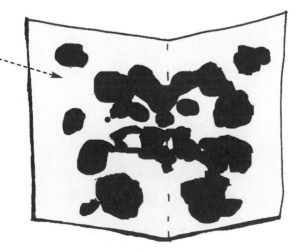

5. Fold the paper again.
   Cut the painted paper
   to look like two wings.

6. Cut out a head and body from the colored paper.

7. Cut two strips for antennae. Curl the tips around the pencil.

Paste the strips onto the back of the head.

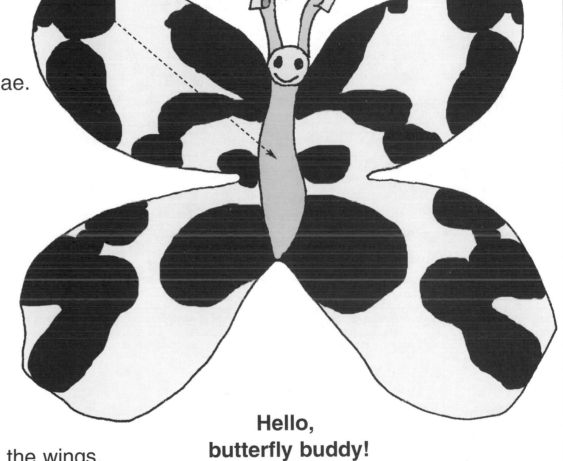

Hello, butterfly buddy!

8. Paste the body between the wings. Draw the face with the marker.

Fancy Fish

Do you like colors?
Then make a fish the fancy way!

Get it!

 Crayons

 White paper

 Watercolor paints

 Paintbrush

 Markers

 Child safety scissors

 Hole punch

 String

Make it!

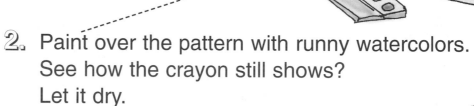

1. Make a crayon pattern on paper.
   Press hard!

2. Paint over the pattern with runny watercolors.
   See how the crayon still shows?
   Let it dry.
   Do the same thing on the back.

3. Fold the paper in half.
   Draw half a fish.
   Cut it out.

4. Cut slits.
   Open up the fish.
   Push the strips in and out.

5. Punch a hole at the top.
   Use the string to hang your fish.

More Fun!

Make your room look like the sea!

1. Make fish in many sizes and shapes.
2. Make a starfish. Make an octopus.
3. Hang them around your room.

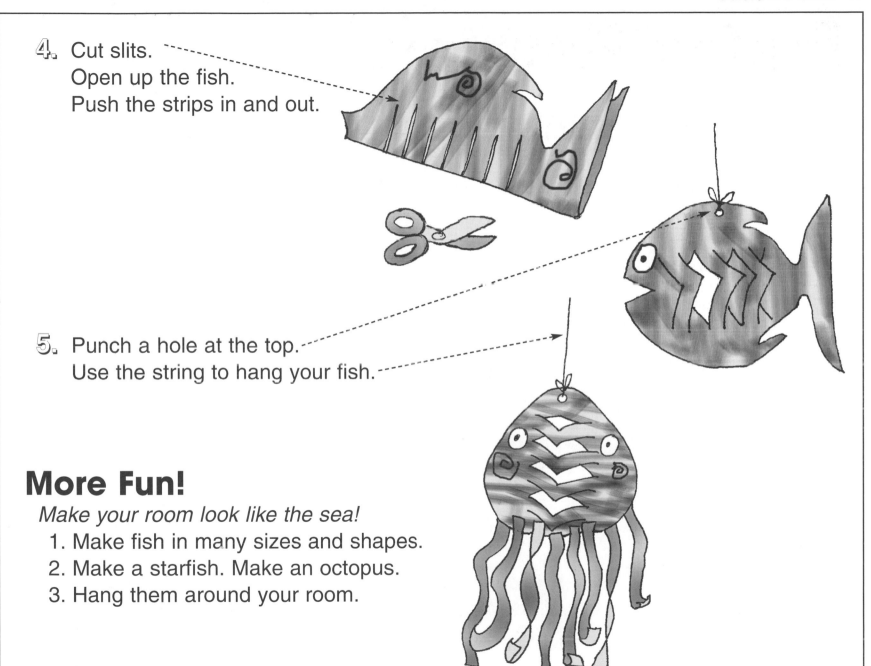

Puffy Paint

Is paint always flat?
Mix this paint and you will see 3-D!

Get it!

 2 tablespoons flour (30 ml)

 2 tablespoons salt (30 ml)

 2 tablespoons water (30 ml)

 Small bowl

 Food coloring

 Squeeze bottle

 Cereal-box cardboard

Make it!

1. Mix flour, salt, and water in the bowl.

2. Add two drops of one color of food coloring.

3. Pour mixture into the squeeze bottle.

4. Make a few colors this way.

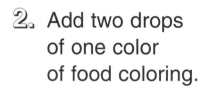

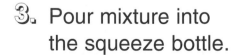

5. Squirt lines, curves,
and dots on the cardboard.

Make a fun picture!

More Fun!

- Paint or draw a picture.
  Outline the shapes
  with puffy paint.

- Write your name
  with puffy paint.

- Cover a box lid with paper.
  Jazz it up with puffy paint.

Curly Dough
Make dough. Now curl it!

Get it!

 2 cups flour
(500 ml)

 1 cup salt
(250 ml)

 1 cup water
(250 ml)

 Mixing bowl

 Food
coloring

 Garlic press

Make it!

1. Put the flour, salt, and water into the mixing bowl.
   Mix it with your hands.

2. Make three balls of dough.
   Add food coloring to each ball.

3. Press each color dough into small balls.

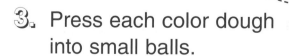

4. Put a ball into the garlic press.
Press the handles.

Wow, curly dough!

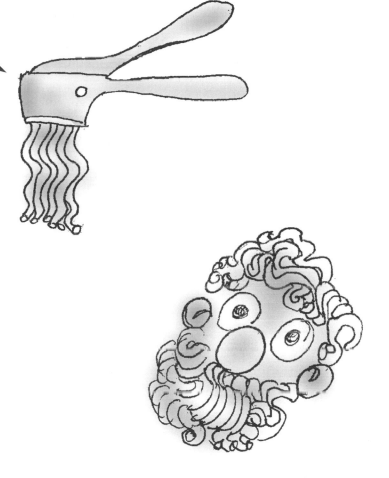

More Fun!

Make more critters!

- Make a lamb.
  Cover it with curly wool.

- Make a face.
  Add curly hair or a curly beard.

- Make a monster.
  Make it hairy and scary.

Art Smart!

- Keep the dough in a zip-locking bag.
- Let your crafts dry hard.

Paper Bowl

It looks like clay, but it's not.
It's really paper!

Get it!

 Cardboard egg carton lid

 2 mixing bowls

 Water

 Flour

 Plastic wrap

 Small bowl

 Tempera paint

 Paintbrush

Make the mash.

1. Tear the egg carton lid into tiny, tiny bits.
   Put the bits in a bowl.

2. Cover the bits with water. Soak overnight.

3. Strain out the water. Squeeze out the water.

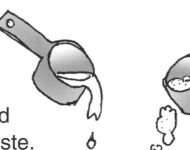

4. Mix ¼ cup (50 ml) flour and ¼ cup (50 ml) water for paste.

5. Mash some paste with your cardboard bits. It will feel like clay.

Make the bowl.

1. Lay plastic wrap inside the small bowl.

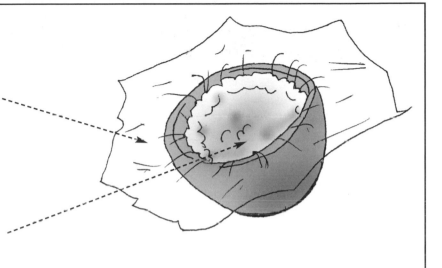

2. Put the mash on top.
   Press to shape the mash like the bowl.
   Let it dry for a day or two.

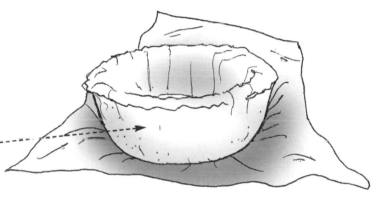

3. Lift out the dry paper bowl.

4. Paint both sides with bright tempera paint.

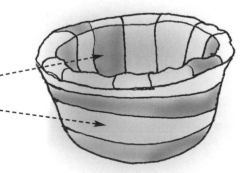

Snappy Snips

Cut and Paste!

If you love to cut and paste,

Snippety-snip.

If you love to cut and paste,

Stickety-stick.

If you love to cut and paste,

Then there isn't time to waste.

Grab your scissors, grab your paste,

Lickety-split!

(To the tune of "If You're Happy and You Know It")

Tail Spin
It's the tail that makes it spin!

Get it!

 Pencil

 Colored paper

 Child safety scissors

 Paste

 Old CD

 Tape

 Hole punch

 String

Make it!

1. Draw a star on the colored paper.
   Cut out the star.

2. Draw a smaller star on different paper.
   Cut it out.
   Paste the small star
   on the big star. - - - - - - - - - -

3. Trace around the CD on paper.
   Mark the center. Put the CD aside.

4. Draw a spiral from
   the center to the edge.
   Cut on the spiral line. - - - - -

5. Punch a hole near the top of the star.

   Tape the spiral to the star. - - - - - -

   Hang it up with string.
   It spins!

Come In

What will your door tag say?

Get it!

Child safety scissors

Colored paper

Markers

Paste

Make it!

1. Cut a shape like this from paper. Cut the slit, too.

2. Use markers to draw a mouth.

3. Cut eyes and ears out of paper. Paste on the eyes and ears.

4. Write words below.

Please knock!
Come in.
Sh-h-h.
Hello.

5. Hang it on a doorknob.

The knob looks like a nose!

More Fun!

What else does the knob look like?

- The sun?
  Paste yellow rays all around.

- A flower?
  Paste petals all around. Add a stem.

- A balloon?
  Paste on string.

Bendy Friend

Make a friend.
Now make her sit, hop, or bend.

Get it!

Markers

Index card

Child safety scissors

Paste

Twist ties

Cardboard scrap

Paper clip*

Make it!

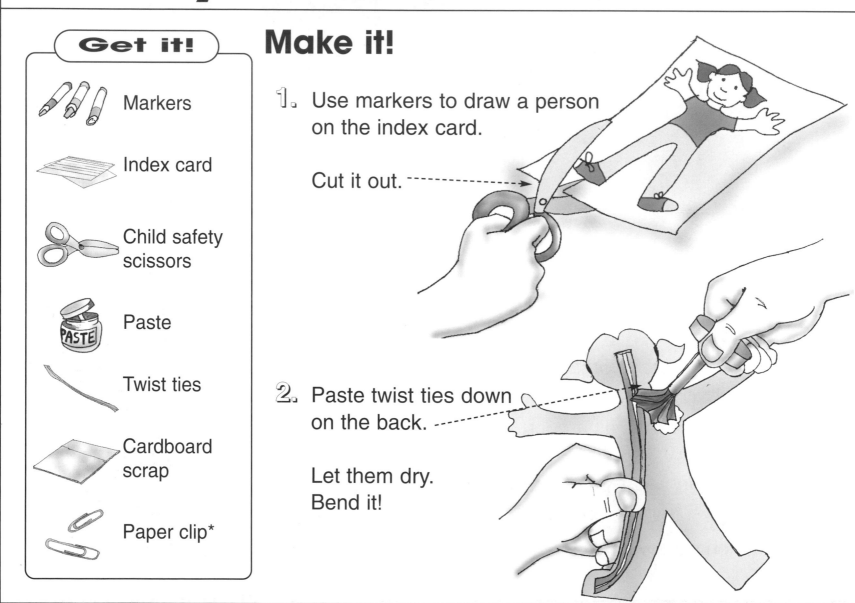

1. Use markers to draw a person on the index card.

   Cut it out. ------>

2. Paste twist ties down on the back. ------

   Let them dry.
   Bend it!

Note: Paper clips cause a poking hazard to children. An adult should control the supply of clips and distribute them as needed.

3. Make a cardboard base.
   Clip a foot to the base.

   Your friend can stand.

You can make a whole family, too.

More Fun!

Make a home for your bendy family.

1. Open up a paper lunch bag.
   Fold down the top.
   Paste it down to make the roof.

2. Use markers to make the bag look like a house.

3. Cut open a door on the door's top and one side.

4. Open the door. Put the bendy family inside.

Lace-Up Book

No need to staple. No need to tie. This pretty book holds with a bow!

Get it!

2 sheets of paper, different colors

Hole punch

Yarn

Child safety scissors

Make it!

1. Hold the two sheets together.
   Fold three times.

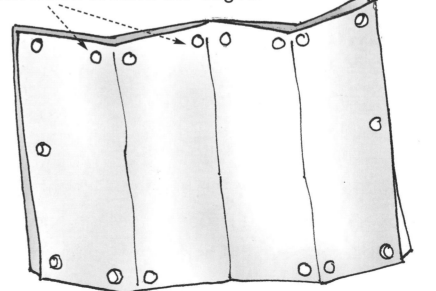

2. Punch holes around the edges.

3. Thread yarn through the holes.
Knot the ends.
Cut off the extra yarn.

4. Use one long tie ------> to close the book.

More Fun!

Now write a little book.

- Love Book:
  Show four things you love.

- My Fish:
  Tell four things about your pet.

- Wish Book:
  Show four wishes.

Itty-Bitty Buzzies

Itty-bitty pets are best!

Get it!

 Child safety scissors

 2 sheets of paper, different colors

 Paste

 Markers

 String

 Twig

Make it!

1. Cut a paper strip of each color. Paste them in an L shape.

2. Fold one strip, then the other like this.

Paste the ends together.

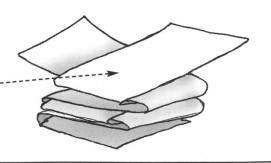

3. Cut out a head.
Draw on a face and antennae.

Cut out two wing shapes.
Paste them on.

Cut strips.
Paste them on for legs.

Paste on a strip for a stinger.
Now it's a bee!

4. Tie string around the middle.

Hang from the twig.
Let it fly!

You can hang many bees on the twig.

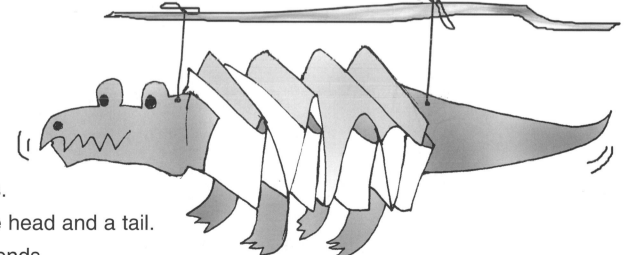

More Fun!

Make a dragon.

1. Use longer strips.
2. Paste on a fierce head and a tail.
3. Hang from both ends.
4. Move the twig to make the dragon glide back and forth.

Book Hooks

Read a good book.
Who will save your place? You can!

Get it!

 Markers

 Colored paper

 Child safety scissors

Make it!

1. Use markers to draw yourself on colored paper. Be sure your arms hang low.

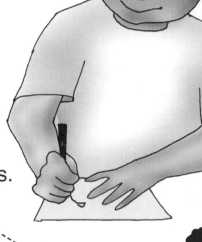

2. Cut the drawing out. Cut the arms with slits like this.

3. Hook yourself to the top of a page.

Read some more.
Then mark your place!

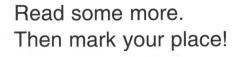

More Fun!

Make a giraffe!
1. Use yellow paper.
2. Make brown spots.
3. Use the legs
   as hooks.

Make an owl!
1. Cut a slit by each wing.
2. Use the wings to
   hold your spot.

Make a cat!
1. Cut a slit by each leg.
2. Do not cut off the card.

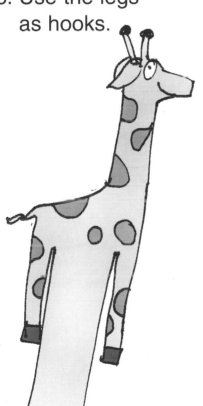

Or, you can make your own critter.
Just be sure to plan how a part will hook onto the page.

Go, Go, Go!

Get on this mini-scooter and ride, ride, ride!

Get it!

 Markers

 Stiff paper

 Child safety scissors

 Tape

 String

 Cereal-box cardboard

Make it!

1. Draw yourself on a scooter. Use markers on stiff paper.

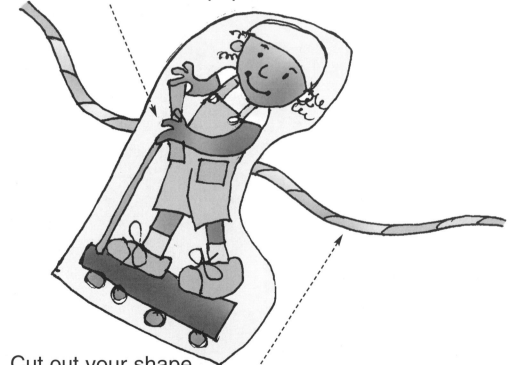

2. Cut out your shape. Tape string to the back.

3. Draw a street on the cardboard.
   Cut a notch on each side for the string.

4. Put the cutout on top
   of the sidewalk.

5. Tie the string around
   the cardboard.

6. Pull the string to make
   the scooter **go, go, go!**

More Fun!

Make your pictures move!

- A rocket zooms in space.
- A butterfly flies in a garden.
- A monkey climbs a tree.

Let's Play!

Play a Game!

Play, play, play a game,

At home or in the sun.

By myself or with a friend,

It is so much fun!

(To the tune of "Row, Row, Row Your Boat")

Fling-A-Ma-Jig

Make a paper-plate gizmo that flies!

Get it!

 Child safety scissors

 2 paper plates

 Glue

 Markers

Make it!

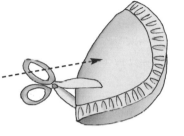

1. Cut out the center of one plate.

2. Put glue all around the edge. Set the uncut plate on top.

3. Use markers to add art.

4. Throw it like a real Frisbee.

Art Smart!
- Bend the plate to start cutting out the center.

Catch-It Cup

It's a game.
What else can it be?

Get it!

 Square of paper

 String

 Bead

 Tape

Make it!

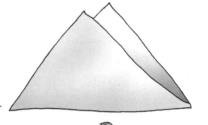

1. Fold the paper in half like this.
   Now it's a triangle. ----------->

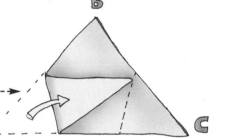

2. Put point B away from you.
   Fold points A and C to ----------->
   the other sides like this.

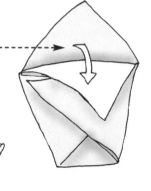

3. Fold one top down. ----------->
   Flip the cup over.

   Fold the other top down.
   Open up the cup. ----------

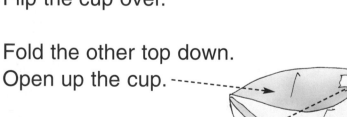

4. Knot a bead on one end of string.
   Tape the other end in the cup. -----

5. Make the cup look like a
   a scary mouth.
   Paste on paper scraps.
   Add eyes.

6. Toss the bead into the air.
   Can you catch it in the cup?

What fun!

More Fun!

Make a basket.
1. Tape a strip to both sides of the cup.
2. Decorate it with markers.

Make a hat.
1. Make the cup from a large
   square of newspaper.
2. Decorate it with markers.
   Put it on your head.

You look great!

Alien Out!

Don't be left with the alien card. Alien out!

Get it!

 11 index cards

 Child safety scissors

 Markers

Draw an alien on one card.

Make it!

1. Cut the index cards in half to make 21 small cards.

2. Draw different people on four cards.

   Draw different animals on four cards.

   Draw different shapes on four cards.

   Draw different flowers on four cards.

   Draw different toys on four cards.

Let's play!

1. Ask one friend to play.
   Mix up the cards.
   Deal five cards.

   Hold cards in a fan.
   Make a pile with the rest.

2. Find matching pairs.
   Put them aside.

   Take a card from the pile
   if you run out.

3. Take turns picking a card
   from each other's hand.
   Put new pairs aside.

4. Are you left with the alien?
   Oh, no!

   Alien out!

Bouncy Buddy

This buddy can go up
and down like a yo-yo!

Get it!

 Stapler

 Toilet-paper
tube

 Beans

 Hole punch

 Child safety
scissors

 Paper scraps

 Markers

 Paste

 Rubber bands

Make it!

1. Staple one end of the tube closed.

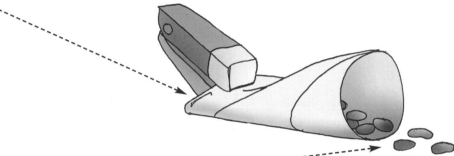

2. Put in a handful of beans.

3. Pinch the top like this.
Punch a hole here.

4. Staple the top closed.

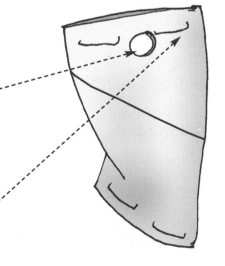

5. Cut paper scraps for the face, arms, and legs.
Use markers to draw the face.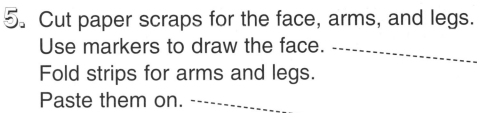
Fold strips for arms and legs.
Paste them on.

6. Loop rubber bands together like this.
Push one through
the hole like this.

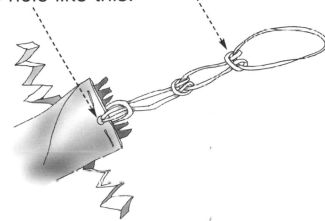

Bounce, bounce, bounce!

More Fun!

What else can bounce?

- A frog.
- A sun.
- Something bright and colorful!

Critter Racers

A dog or a frog? A cat or a bat?
Who will win the race?

Get it!

 Markers

 Cereal-box cardboard

 Child safety scissors

 Hole punch

 String

 Ruler

Make it!

1. Draw a critter on the cardboard.

2. Cut it out.
   Punch a hole near the top.

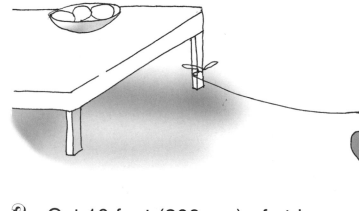

3. Cut 10 feet (300 cm) of string.
   Tie one end to a table leg.
   Thread string through the hole.

   A friend can make a critter, too!

Race Time!

Critters can race back and forth. Make a finish line.

1. Pull the string tight. The critter will stand.

2. Let the string hang loose.
   The critter will flop.

3. Stand — flop — stand — flop
   moves the critter along.

   A rug makes
   a good racetrack.

   A smooth floor makes
   a tricky racetrack.

   Who won?

More Fun!

- Frogs make good racers.
  So do turtles, rabbits, cars, or people.

- Make many.
  Pick the one to win the race.

Monster Mouth

Feed this hungry monster to win!

Get it!

 Markers

 Paper grocery bag

 Child safety scissors

 Stapler

 Old newspapers

 Old magazine

 Rubber bands

Make the monster.

1. Draw a monster face on the bag. Use markers to make it weird.

2. Cut silly ears. Do not cut off. Bend them forward.

   Cut a funny nose. Bend it up.

   Cut out a big mouth, all the way around. Remove it.

3. Fringe the hair at the top. Staple the top shut.

   A friend can make a monster, too!

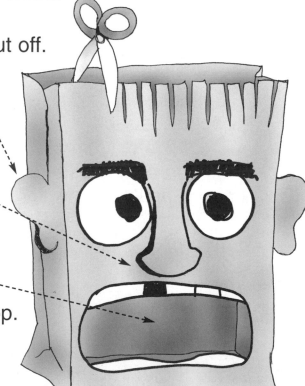

Make the food.

1. Crumple a page of newspaper into a ball.

Wrap it in a bright magazine page.

2. Hold it on with rubber bands.

3. Make a few food balls this way.

Let's Play!

1. Try to throw the balls into the monster's mouth.

2. Take turns with a friend.
Who can feed the most food to the monster?

Tricky-Tac-Toe

Move three in a row to win!

Get it!

 Child safety scissors

 Cereal-box cardboard

 Ruler

 Markers

 Colored paper

 Paste

 6 milk jug lids

Make the board!

1. Cut out a cardboard square 6" x 6" (15 x 15 cm).

   Trace the square onto colored paper.

   Now cut out the paper square. Paste it on the cardboard.

2. Cut out four thin paper strips 8" (20 cm) long.

   Paste them down to make nine squares.

Make the pieces.

1. Trace around a lid three times in one color. Do it again in another color.

   Decorate them in different ways, such as three cats and three yellow stars — your choice.

2. Cut out the circles. Pop them into the lids.

Let's Play!

1. Take turns setting out the pieces. Try to place three in a row.

2. No winner yet? Take turns moving pieces from one square to the next.

The winner puts three in a row.

More Fun!

Play Tic-Tac-Toe!

1. Each player needs five pieces.
2. No moving this time!

For You and Me

Presents!

I can make a gift for you,

Gift for you,

Gift for you.

I can give a gift to you.

Happy Birthday!

Last line choices:

Merry Christmas!
Happy Hanukkah!
Happy Father's Day!
Happy Mother's Day!
You're my special friend!

(To the tune of "London Bridge Is Falling Down")

Plate Puzzle

Make a puzzle. Then mix it up.

Get it!

 Markers

 2 paper plates

 Child safety scissors

Make it!

1. Color a picture on a paper plate.

2. Cut it into puzzle shapes.

3. Put the mixed-up pieces on a new paper plate.

More Fun!

Make silly puzzle people!
Start with index cards and markers.

1. Draw three kinds of heads on three cards.

2. Draw three kinds of bodies on three cards.

3. Draw three kinds of legs on three cards.

4. Now mix and match the parts.

Can you put these mixed-up pictures back together?

Peacock Fan
It's a colorful fan to keep you cool!

Get it!

 Markers

 Paper

 Paste

 Child safety scissors

Make it!

1. Decorate the paper.
   Fold it back and forth.

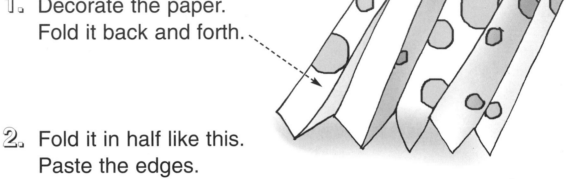

2. Fold it in half like this.
   Paste the edges.

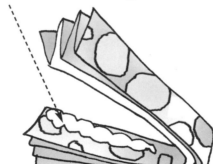

3. Draw a peacock body.
   Draw feet and a face.

4. Cut the body out.
Paste it on the fan.

It's fan-tastic!

More Fun!

Color the folds like a rainbow!

1. Thread yarn through the bottom.

2. Tie it in a bow for a rainbow fan.

Make a snowflake fan!

1. Make little snips on the folds.

2. Try different shapes and sizes.

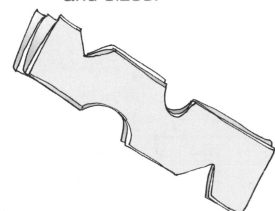

Make a circle hanger!

1. Paste four fans together.

2. Hang from a string.

Flutter Flier

This butterfly flutters in the wind!

Get it!

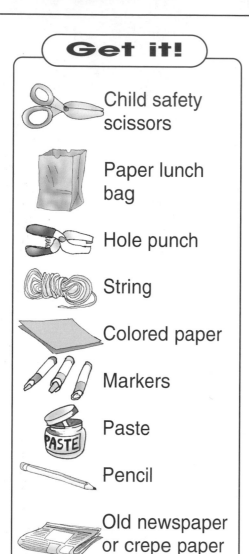

- Child safety scissors
- Paper lunch bag
- Hole punch
- String
- Colored paper
- Markers
- Paste
- Pencil
- Old newspaper or crepe paper

Make it!

1. Cut the bottom from a bag.

   Fold down the top.
   Punch two holes at the top.

   Thread string through the holes.
   Tie the ends in a knot.

2. Cut out two wing shapes with tabs.

   Decorate them with markers.

   Paste the tabs to the sides of the bag.

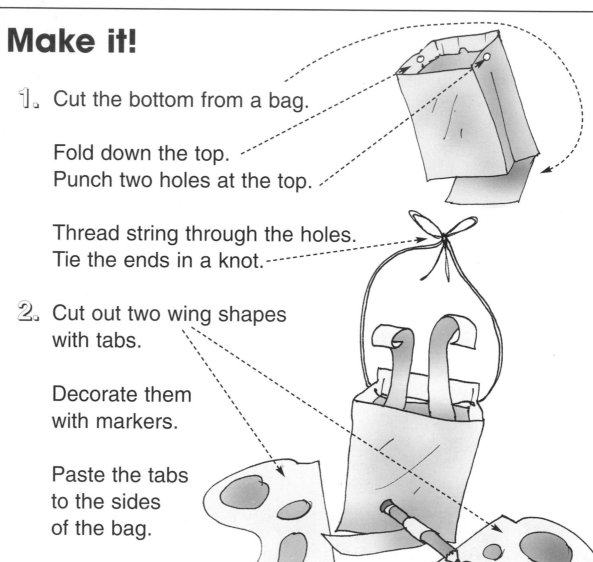

3. Cut out a butterfly body shape.
   Paste it on the bag.

4. Cut two paper strips for antennae.
   Curl the tips around a pencil.

   Paste them onto the body.

5. Cut newspaper strips.
   Paste along the bottom.
   Hang the Flutter Flier outside.

   Watch it flutter in the wind.

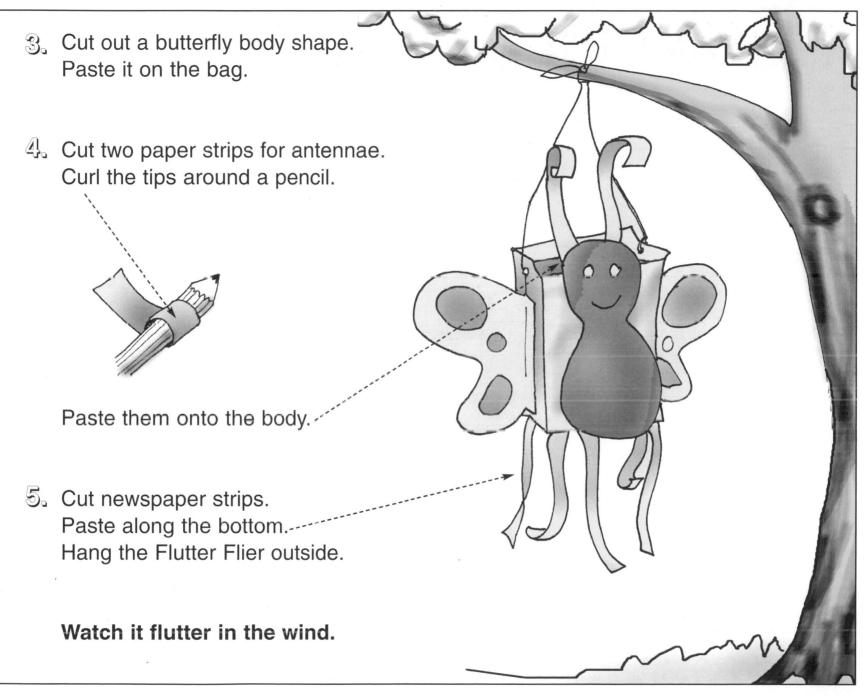

Happy Pop-Up Card

Wish someone a "happy day" the pop-up way!

Get it!

 Colored paper

 Markers

 Child safety scissors

Paste

Make it!

1. Fold the paper in half to make a card. Draw a pretty picture on the front.

2. Cut a thin strip of paper. Fold it back and forth to make the pop-up spring.

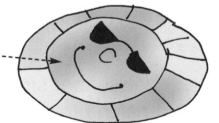

3. Use markers to make a decoration. Cut it out.

4. Paste one end of the spring to the inside of the card.

   Paste the other end to your decoration.

5. Write your message in the card.

More Fun!

Make a friend happy!

- You are out of this world!
  Make a springy rocket.

- Happy Birthday!
  Make a springy cake.

- Have a lucky day!
  Make a springy rainbow.

  What's your idea?

Light Bright

Hang this banner in front of a window!

Get it!

Child safety scissors

Paper

Yarn

Paste

Crayons

Cooking oil

Cotton ball

Make it!

1. Cut a banner shape
   from paper.
   Fold the top over
   a long piece of yarn.
   Paste it down.
   Tie the yarn in a bow.

2. Draw a pretty picture
   with crayons.
   Press hard.
   Fill the paper with color.

3. Put oil on
   the cotton ball.
   Rub the oil over
   the picture.

   Let it dry.

4. Hang it in the light.

More Fun!

- Cut any shape you like.
- Draw a holiday picture.
- Add glitter or punch holes along the edges.

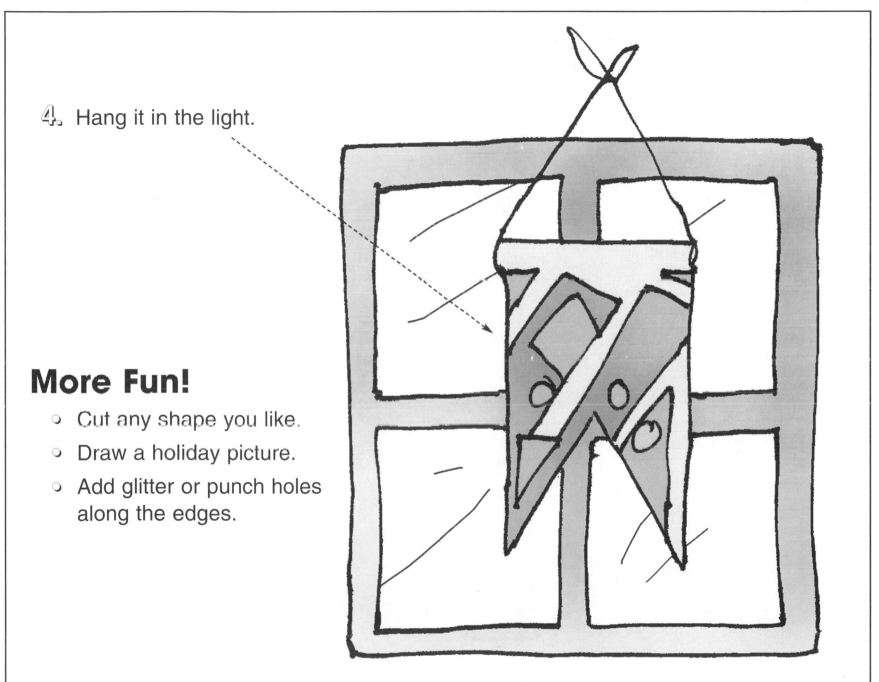

Desk Set

Leave a note. It's easy with this desk set.

Get it!

 Crayons

 Large sheet of paper

 Watercolor paints

 Paintbrush

 Cereal-box cardboard

 Ruler

 Stapler

 Child safety scissors

 Paste

 Sheets of white paper

 Empty juice can

Decorate the paper!

1. Make a crayon rubbing of textures: bark, leaves, rugs, tile — whatever you can think of.

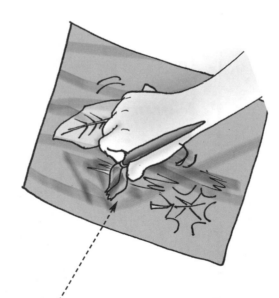

2. Paint over it with watercolor. Let it dry.

Make the pad.

1. Fold over the top 1" (2.5 cm) of the cereal-box cardboard. Staple the ends.

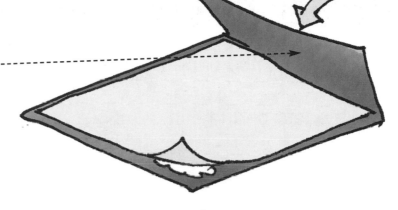

2. Cut two pieces out of the painted paper.

   Paste them here and here.

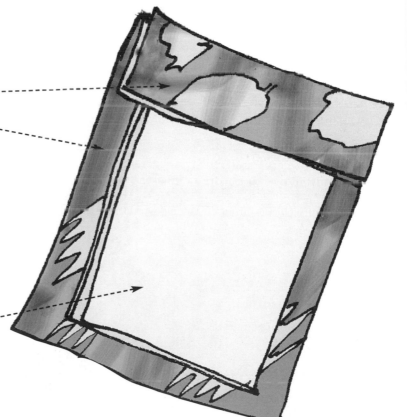

3. Fold the sheets of white paper in half. Fold in half again. Cut on the folds. Fill your pad with the paper.

Make the pencil holder!

1. Cut the painted paper to cover the can.

2. Rub paste on the can.

3. Wrap your paper around the can. Press it on.

Fast Frame

Frame a photo.
Frame your picture. Frame it fast!

Get it!

 Markers

 Colored
paper scraps

 Sheet of
white paper

 Paste

 Hole punch

 Large sheet
of paper

 Yarn

Make it!

1. Draw a picture or make one
with paper scraps on the white paper.

2. Paste it in the center of a larger piece of paper.

3. Fold up each edge. Pinch the corners.

4. Punch two holes at the top.

5. Thread yarn
through the holes.

Tie the ends
in a knot.

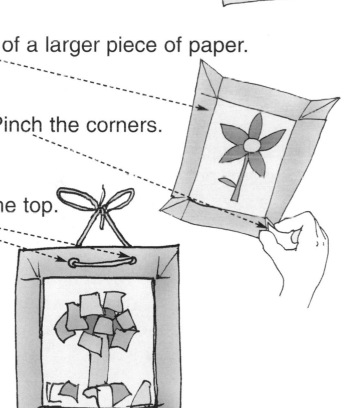

Let's Pretend

Who am I?

I'm a puppy, see my ears,
Floppy ears, floppy ears.
I'm a puppy, see my ears,
I'm a puppy today.

I'm a wizard, see my wand,
Magic wand, magic wand.
I'm a wizard, see my wand,
I'm a wizard today.

I'm a butterfly, see my wings,
Fluttering wings, fluttering wings.
I'm a butterfly, see my wings,
Watch me fly away.

(To the tune of "Here We Go 'Round the Mulberry Bush")

Top Hat

Wear a smile (or a frown) on top of your head!

Get it!

 Child safety scissors

 Paper grocery bag

 Tempera paint

 Paintbrush

 Section of old newspaper

 Stapler

Put on your big top hat and surprise everyone!

Make it!

1. Cut open the paper bag, so it lies flat.

2. Paint on a scary face, a sad face, or a happy face in the middle.
   You can cut out ears and pop them out.

3. Cut newspaper strips for silly hair.
   Staple them around the top of the bag.

4. Staple the bag to fit your head.

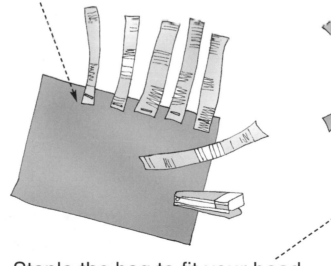

Wake-Up Puppet

Wake up.
It's time for the show!

Get it!

 Child safety scissors

 Colored paper scraps

 Paste

 Paper lunch bag

 Markers

Make it!

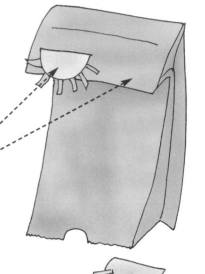

1. Cut and paste closed-eye shapes from the paper scraps.

   Paste them on the bag here.

2. Cut and paste open-eye shapes from paper scraps.

   Paste them on the bag here.

3. Use paper scraps and markers to decorate your puppet. Add paper arms.

4. Put your hand inside the bag.

Close your hand for closed eyes.

Open your hand for open eyes.

**Anyone or any critter can sleep —
and then wake up!**

More Fun!

Make puppet show characters!

- Goldilocks sleeps; the bears wake her up.
- Rip van Winkle sleeps; he wakes up 100 years later!
- A bear sleeps all winter long, but wakes up in the spring!

Wing Fling

Give yourself wings. Now fly away!

Get it!

 Child safety scissors

 Paper grocery bag

 Tempera paint
red   blue

 Paintbrush

 Hole punch

 Stapler

 String

Make it!

1. Cut open the paper bag.
   Fold it in half.
   Trace this wing shape.

   Cut out the wings.

2. Unfold the bag.
   Paint both sides of both wings
   in pretty butterfly colors.
   Let them dry.

3. Punch holes in four spots.

4. Tuck here and staple.

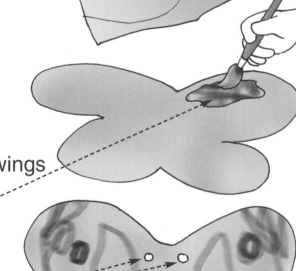

5. Thread a very long piece of string through the holes.

Tie a knot.

6. Slip your arms into the string and fly away!

More Fun!

Who has wings?

- A butterfly
- A fairy
- A bat
- A dragonfly

Just think of all the fliers you can be!

Silly Crown

With a silly crown, you can be whatever you want to be!

Get it!

 Child safety scissors

 Paper

 Colored paper scraps

 Paste

 Stapler

Make it!

1. Cut a long piece of a paper that can fit around your head.

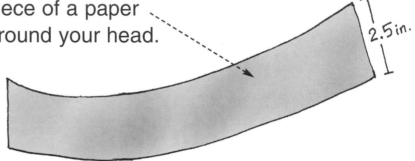

2.5 in.

2. Make a dog face with paper scraps. Paste it on the center of the headband.

3. Cut out long dog ears.

   Paste one on each side.

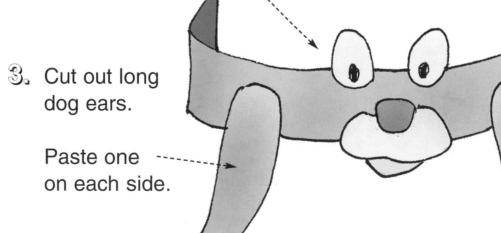

4. Staple the band to fit your head.

More Fun!

Be a garden!

1. Snip a green band to look like grass.

2. Make flowers and bugs from paper scraps.
   Paste them onto the grass.

3. Staple the band to fit your head.

Be the ocean!

1. Cut a blue band to look like waves.

2. Make a boat shape.
   Paste it on the center of the band.

3. Staple the band to fit your head.

Wonder Wand

Do you believe in magic?
Then make a wonder wand!

Get it!

 Colored paper

 Pencil

 Paste

 Child safety scissors

 Clean, empty potato chip bag

 Markers

Make it!

1. Wrap paper around a pencil like this. Paste down the end.

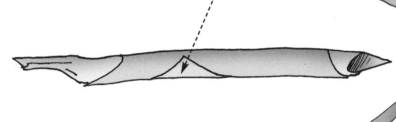

2. Cut a piece from the chip bag. Fringe it like this.

3. Paste the fringe around the tip of the wand.

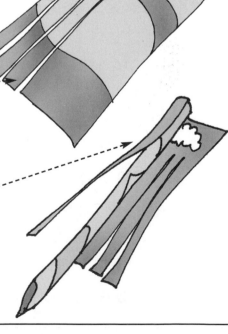

4. Cut out two stars.
Decorate them with markers.

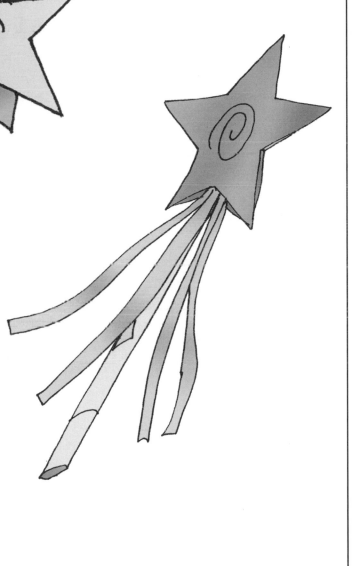

5. Paste them onto the wand.

Use your wand for pretend, dreams, and wishes.

More Fun!

More wand decorations!

- How about the sun?
- The moon?
- A lightning bolt?

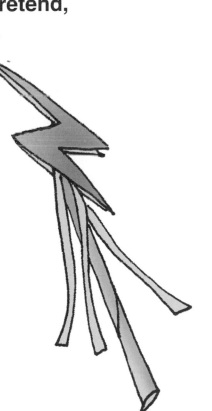

Finger-Fun Puppets

What can your fingers be?

Get it!

 Child safety scissors

 Index card

 Markers

Make it!

1. Cut the card to look like a mouse. Decorate it with markers.

2. Cut a thin strip and a hole at the back.

3. Poke your finger through the hole.

Wiggle it like a tail!

More Fun!

Think of all the silly things your fingers can be!

- Rabbit ears
- Elephant's trunk
- Spider legs

Art Smart!

- Trace a dime for the hole.

Tiny Theater

A tissue box is a tiny theater. Let the play begin!

Get it!

 Scissors for grown-up use only

 Empty rectangular tissue box

 White paper

 Markers

 Child safety scissors

 Index cards

 Tape

 Drinking straws

Make the stage!

1. Ask a grown-up to help you cut the box like this.

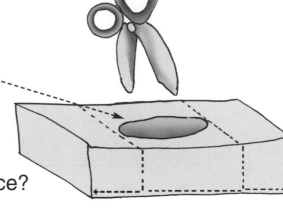

Make the setting!

Where does the show take place? It's called the setting.

1. Fold the white paper so it hangs down the back of the stage.

2. Use markers to draw the setting on the paper.

If the place changes, hang a new setting.

Make the puppets!

Who are the stars of the show?

1. Cut the index cards in half.
   Use one half for each puppet.

2. Draw each character with markers.

3. Tape a straw to the back of each one,
   so the straw sticks out at the top
   of each puppet.

Show time!

Tell a favorite story or make up your own.

1. Change the setting to match
   where it happens.

2. Hold the puppets in front
   of the setting.

3. Use different voices
   for each puppet.

Colorful Music

Make Some Music!

Listen to my drumbeat: rat-tat-tat, rat-tat-tat, rat-tat-tat.
Listen to my drumbeat: rat-tat-tat.
Play along with me.

Listen to my maracas: ch-ch-ch, ch-ch-ch, ch-ch-ch.
Listen to my maracas: ch-ch-ch.
Play along with me.

Listen to my kalimba: twang-twang-twang, twang-twang-twang,
twang-twang-twang.
Listen to my kalimba: twang-twang- twang.
Play along with me.

(To the tune of "Buffalo Gals")

Shake, Rattle & Roll

Sing a song and shake, shake, shake.

Get it!

 Tempera paint

 Paintbrush

 Toilet-paper tube

 Stapler

 Rice or beans

Make it!

1. Paint a bright pattern on the tube.

2. Pinch one end of the tube. Staple closed.

3. Put in a handful of beans.

4. Pinch the other end of the tube. Staple it closed.

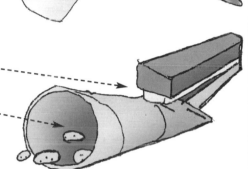

Now, shake, rattle, and roll!

More Fun!

Make fringe!

1. Cut long strips from a clean, empty potato chip bag.
2. Staple around the bottom.

Rat-Tat-Tat

Twist the stick.
Swing the beads. Rat-tat-tat!

 **Get it!**

 Markers

 2 small
paper plates

 Colored paper

Pencil

 Paste

 Tape

Beads

 String

 Glue

The art part!

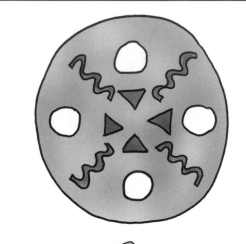

1. Mark four parts on each plate.

2. Use markers to draw
the same shapes
in each part.

3. Wrap paper around
a pencil like this.

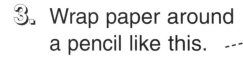

Paste down the
end of the paper.

Tape the stick to the plate.

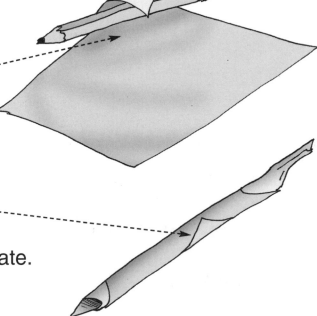

4. Knot beads onto the ends of the string.
Tape the string to the back of one plate.

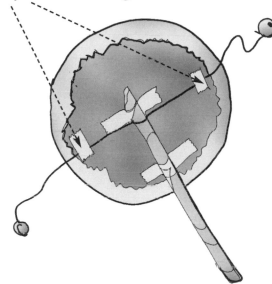

5. Put glue around the edge
of the other plate.

Press the two plates together.
Let them dry.

Turn the handle this way, then that.
The beads hit the plates.

Rat-tat-tat.

Rain Stick

Slow the flow. It sounds like rain.

Get it!

 Markers

 Paper

 Paste

 Clean, empty potato chip can

 Foil

 Rice

 Child safety scissors

 Clean plastic grocery bag

 Tape

Make it!

1. Decorate the paper. Paste it on the can.

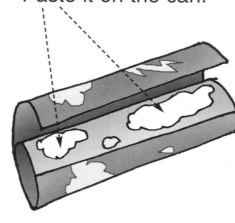

2. Crumple the foil. Put it in the can.

3. Add a handful of rice. Snap on the lid.

4. Cut fringe from the plastic bag.
Tape it around the top of the can.

5. Slowly rock the can.

What do you hear?

More Fun!

Name the sound!

○ Does it sound like rain?
Make a rainy picture.

○ Does it sound like wind?
Make a windy picture.

○ Does it sound like a train?
Make a train picture.

Pling Thing

Sing and pling on your Pling Thing.

Get it!

 Child safety scissors

 Colored paper

 Paste

 Tissue box

 Rubber bands in all sizes: thick, thin, long, short

Make it!

1. Cut paper strips.
   Paste them around the box.

2. Snip the strips along the opening of the box.

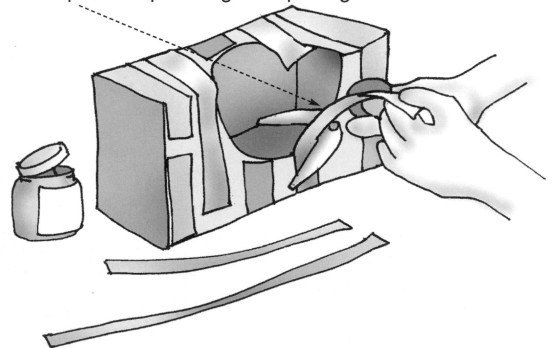

3. Paste bright paper inside the box.

4. Stretch rubber bands across the opening.

5. Pluck the strings.

   Pling, pling, pling.

More Fun!

○ Try other box shapes. Does the sound change?

Critter Call

A hen? An owl?
What makes this sound?

Get it!

- Pen
- Paper cup
- 3 feet (90 cm) of string
- Paper clip*
- Markers
- Paper scraps
- Child safety scissors
- Paste

Make it!

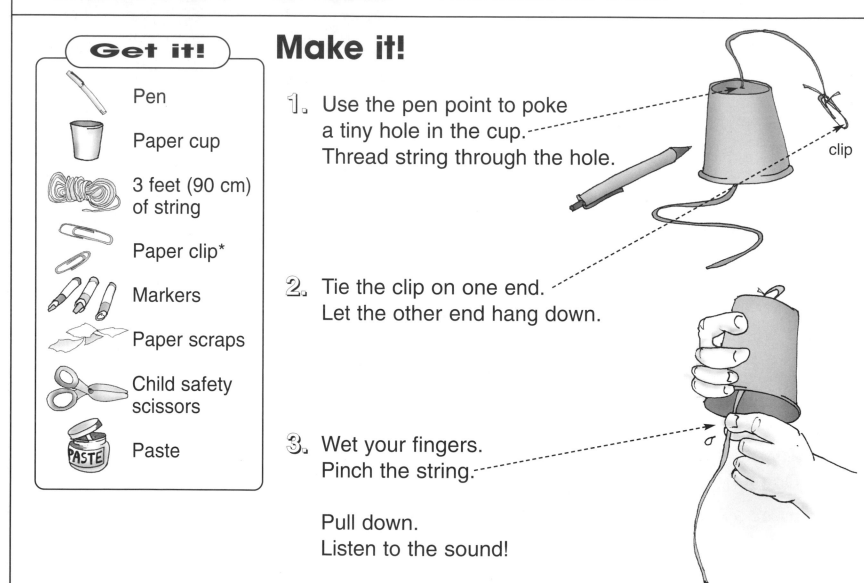

1. Use the pen point to poke a tiny hole in the cup. Thread string through the hole.

    clip

2. Tie the clip on one end. Let the other end hang down.

3. Wet your fingers. Pinch the string.

    Pull down. Listen to the sound!

*Note: Paper clips cause a poking hazard to children. An adult should control the supply of clips and distribute them as needed.

4. Use markers and paper scraps to decorate the cup.

Can you make it look like the critter that makes the sound?

More Fun!

Make a duck, a lion or a monster!

○ They all make fun sounds!

Kazoo

Sing a song and shake, shake, shake.

Get it!

 Hole punch

 Toilet-paper tube

 Glue

 Bright yarn

 Waxed paper

 Crayons

 Rubber band

Make it!

1. Punch a hole in the tube.

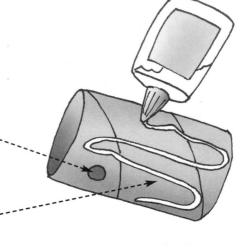

2. Cover the tube with glue.

3. Wind yarn around the tube in rows. Don't cover the hole.

Press the yarn into the glue. Let it dry.

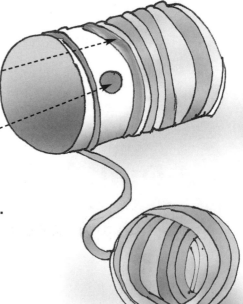

4. Color the waxed paper
with bright crayons.

5. Use a rubber band to hold
the waxed paper on one end.

6. Hum into the open end.

Hum a happy kazoo song!

Kalimba

Play this African piano with your thumbs.

Get it!

Thick cardboard, about 3" x 6" (7.5 x 15 cm)

Crayons

Small paper clips*

Big paper clips*

Make it!

1. Cover the cardboard with bright colors.
Press hard.

2. Cover the bright colors with black crayon.
Press hard.

3. Bend all of your paper clips like this.

4. Use one of the paper clips to scratch a design on the black cardboard.

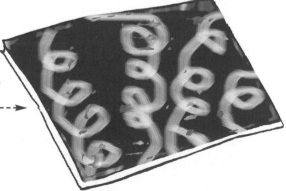

5. Slide the clips into the holes on the edge of the cardboard like this.

6. Bend them up a little.

Make music!

1. Hold the kalimba.
2. Use your thumbs to press down on the clips.

Twang, twang, twang!
What cool sounds!

Wearable Art

All Day Long!

Hannah wore bright bangles,
Bright bangles, bright bangles.
Hannah wore bright bangles,
All day long.

Nicholas wore his zoo bag,
Zoo bag, zoo bag.
Nicholas wore his zoo bag,
All day long.

Emily wore charming charms,
Charming charms, charming charms.
Emily wore charming charms,
All day long.

(To the tune of "Mary Wore a Red Dress")

Zoo Bags

You can smile. This little lion can, too!
You can hold things. It can, too!

Get it!

Colored paper

Child safety scissors

Markers

Hole punch

Yarn

Make it!

1. Fold the paper in half. Cut out two shapes at the same time.

2. Draw a happy lion's face on one shape.

3. Punch holes around three sides.

4. Thread yarn in and out of the holes. Tie the ends to make a strap.

5. Hang the bag around your neck.

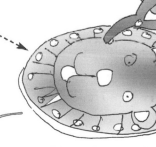

No holes on this side.

Zigzag Wear

Pick two colors you like best.
Now zigzag them!

Get it!

 2 sheets of
paper,
different colors

 Child safety
scissors

 Paste

 Hole punch

 Rubber bands

Make the dangle!

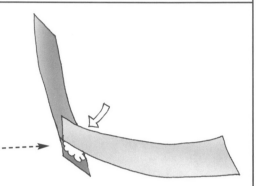

1. Cut a strip of each color.

   Paste them in an L shape. ----------→

2. Fold one strip, ----------→
   then the other like this.

   Paste the ends together. ↰

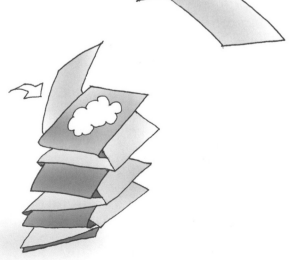

3. Punch a hole at the tip.

4. Loop a rubber band through the hole.

5. Make another dangle just like the first.
Slip the bands over your ears.

The zigzag look is so hip!

Make the bangle!

1. Make a longer band from folded strips.

2. Paste the ends to make a circle.

3. Slide it over your hand.

Bead It!

Roll paper into beads. It's a quick trick!

Get it!

Child safety scissors

Colored paper

Ruler

Paste

Drinking straw

Hole punch

String

Presto! You've made beads!

Make the beads.

1. Cut a paper strip as long as a straw and 3" (7.5 cm) wide.

2. Fold it in half.
   Open it and cover it with paste.

3. Put a straw on the fold.
   Fold the strip in half.
   Press hard.
   Let it dry.

4. Snip the strip into shapes.

3"

punch hole

fold

press paper

Make the jewelry!

Make a necklace, bracelet, or headband.

1. Make many beads this way.
   Make many colors.
   Make many shapes.

2. You can punch holes in them.

3. Thread string through the beads.

4. Knot the ends together.

Wow! That's nice!

Wrap tape around tip of string.

zigzag bead

fold paper

More Fun!

You can add a zigzag between beads!

1. Fold a paper strip back and forth.
2. Punch a hole at each fold.
3. Thread the string through the hole.

Charming Charms
Hang fun photos on your wrist!

Get it!

 Paper clips*

 Child safety scissors

 Index cards

 Hole punch

 Magazine

 Paste

Make it!

1. Link clips to fit your wrist.

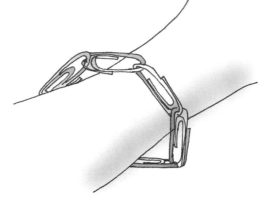

2. Cut charm shapes from index cards. Punch a hole at the top. - - - - - - - - - - - ->

3. Find tiny, fun photos in a magazine.
Cut them out.
Paste them to both sides of the shapes.

Note: Paper clips cause a poking hazard to children. An adult should control the supply of clips and distribute them as needed.

4. Slip the charms onto the bracelet.

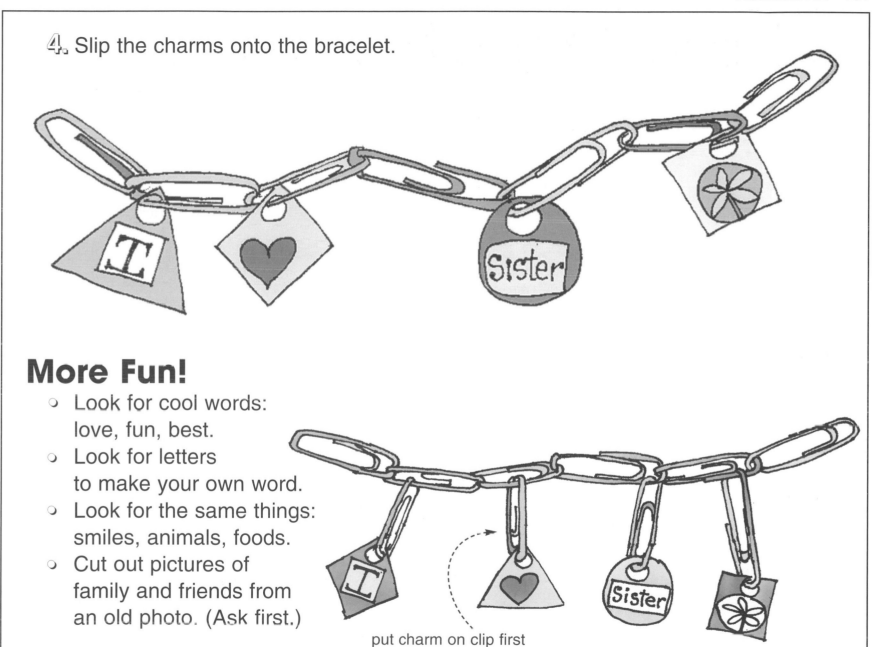

More Fun!

- Look for cool words: love, fun, best.
- Look for letters to make your own word.
- Look for the same things: smiles, animals, foods.
- Cut out pictures of family and friends from an old photo. (Ask first.)

put charm on clip first

Iguana Necklace
Wear a pet around your neck.

Get it!

 Pencil

 Colored paper

 Child safety scissors

 Hole punch

 Drinking straw

 Yarn

Make it!

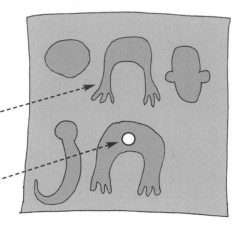

1. Think of the pet's parts. Draw them on colored paper.

   Cut them out. Punch a hole at the top of each part.

2. Cut a straw into small beads.

3. Lay the parts out in order with the head on top.

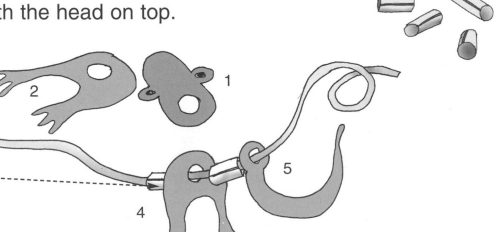

Put a straw bead between each one.

4. Thread yarn through your pet and the beads.

5. Hang on your neck.

Your pet wiggles as you walk!

More Fun!

Try the Iguana.
Then make your own pet!

Art Smart!

- A tab will turn a body part the right way
  See the iguana head and tail.

Paper Lei

Say "aloha" with this lovely lei (sounds like *lay*).

Get it!

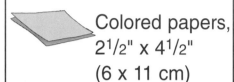 Colored papers, 2¹/₂" x 4¹/₂" (6 x 11 cm)

 Child safety scissors

Paste

Yarn

Make it!

1. Fold a small paper in half.

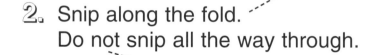

2. Snip along the fold. Do not snip all the way through.

3. Unfold it and roll into a tube.

4. Paste the ends together.

   Push and pinch it open.

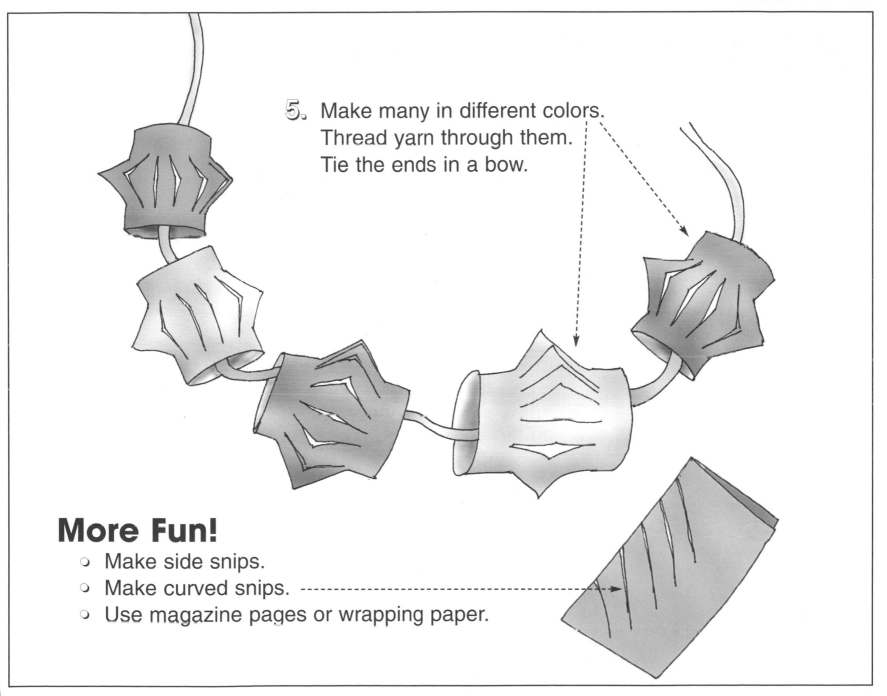

5. Make many in different colors.
Thread yarn through them.
Tie the ends in a bow.

More Fun!

- Make side snips.
- Make curved snips.
- Use magazine pages or wrapping paper.

Bangles

Pick two colors you like best.
One is on top. One shows through.

Get it!

 Child safety scissors

 Toilet-paper tube

 2 sheets of paper, different colors

 Paste

 Paper

Make it!

1. Cut the tube like this for three bangle bases.

2. Cut six strips 1½" x 6½" (3.5 x 16 cm) in two colors.

3. Snip designs in one strip. Paste it on top of the other strip.

4. Paste the paper band on top of the base. Paste the band tips over the ends of the base.

5. Slip the bangle on your arm. Very nice!

6. Make paper bands for the other bases. Paste them on.

More Fun!

Make bangle bases.

1. Fold the paper strip in half.
2. Snip on the fold like this.
3. Open up the paper.
   Fold the fin shapes back.
4. Paste on top of a new color.

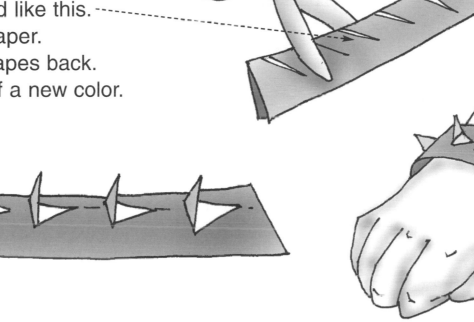

More Fun!

Make more bangle bases.

1. Fold the paper strip in half.
2. Snip shapes on the fold.
3. Unfold the strip.
4. Paste the strip on a new color.
5. Save the tiny paper shapes.
   Paste on top of a new color.

Index

Williamson's *Little Hands* Books

The following **Little Hands**® books for ages 2 to 7 are 128 to 160 pages,
fully illustrated, trade paper, 10 x 8, $12.95 US.

AT THE ZOO!
Explore the Animal World with Craft Fun
by Judy Press

• • •

Parents' Choice Gold Award
FUN WITH MY 5 SENSES
Activities to Build Learning Readiness
by Sarah A. Williamson

• • •

Little Hands **FINGERPLAYS & ACTION SONGS**
Seasonal Activities & Creative Play
for 2- to 6-Year-Olds
by Emily Stetson & Vicky Congdon

• • •

AROUND-THE-WORLD ART & ACTIVITIES
Visiting the 7 Continents through Craft Fun
by Judy Press

Little Hands **PAPER PLATE CRAFTS**
Creative Art Fun for 3- to 7-Year-Olds
by Laura Check

• • •

Real Life Award
The Little Hands **ART BOOK**
Exploring Arts & Crafts with 2- to 6-Year-Olds
by Judy Press

• • •

The Little Hands **PLAYTIME! BOOK**
50 Activities to Encourage Cooperation & Sharing
by Regina Curtis

American Bookseller Pick of the Lists
RAINY DAY PLAY!
Explore, Create, Discover, Pretend
by Nancy Fusco Castaldo

• • •

Parents' Choice Approved
Early Childhood News Directors' Choice Award
SHAPES, SIZES & MORE SURPRISES!
A Little Hands Early Learning Book
by Mary Tomczyk

• • •

ARTSTARTS for Little Hands!
Fun Discoveries for 3- to 7-Year-Olds
by Judy Press

• • •

Parents' Choice Approved
The Little Hands **NATURE BOOK**
Earth, Sky, Critters & More
by Nancy Fusco Castaldo

• • •

MATH PLAY!
80 Ways to Count & Learn
by Diane McGowan & Mark Schrooten

• • •

Parent's Guide Children's Media Award
ALPHABET ART
With A to Z Animal Art & Fingerplays
by Judy Press

• • •

Parents' Choice Approved
The Little Hands **BIG FUN CRAFT BOOK**
Creative Fun for 2- to 6-Year-Olds
by Judy Press

Williamson's *Kids Can!*® Books

The following Williamson *Kids Can!*® books for ages 7 to 13 are each 144 to 176 pages,
fully illustrated, trade paper, 11 x 8¹/₂, $12.95 US.

THE KIDS' WILDLIFE BOOK
**Exploring Animal Worlds through
Indoor/Outdoor Crafts & Experiences**
by Warner Shedd

• • •

Early Childhood News Directors' Choice Award
Real Life Award
VROOM! VROOM!
Making 'dozers, 'copters, trucks & more
by Judy Press

• • •

Parents' Choice Gold Award
Benjamin Franklin Best Juvenile Nonfiction Award
KIDS MAKE MUSIC!
Clapping and Tapping from Bach to Rock
by Avery Hart and Paul Mantell

• • •

American Bookseller Pick of the Lists
Parents' Choice Approved
Oppenheim Toy Portfolio Best Book Award
SUMMER FUN!
60 Activities for a Kid-Perfect Summer
by Susan Williamson

• • •

Parents' Choice Honor Award
THE KIDS' NATURAL HISTORY BOOK
Making Dinos, Fossils, Mammoths & More!
by Judy Press

• • •

KIDS COOK!
Fabulous Food for the Whole Family
by Sarah Williamson & Zachary Williamson

Parents' Choice Recommended
KIDS' ART WORKS!
Creating with Color, Design, Texture & More
b y Sandi Henry

• • •

Parents' Choice Approved
KIDS CREATE!
Art & Craft Experiences for 3- to 9-Year-Olds
by Laurie Carlson

• • •

Parents' Choice Recommended
THE KIDS' BOOK OF WEATHER FORECASTING
Build a Weather Station, "Read" the Sky & Make Predictions!
with meteorologist Mark Breen & Kathleen Friestad

• • •

The Kids' Guide to FIRST AID
All about Bruises, Burns, Stings, Sprains & Other Ouches
by Karen Buhler Gale, R.N.

• • •

The Kids' Guide to
MAKING SCRAPBOOKS & PHOTO ALBUMS!
How to Collect, Design, Assemble, Decorate
by Laura Check

• • •

JAZZY JEWELRY
Power Beads, Crystals, Chokers, & Illusion and Tattoo Styles
by Diane Baker

• • •

American Bookseller Pick of the Lists
Parents' Choice Recommended
ADVENTURES IN ART
Arts & Crafts Experiences for 8- to 13-Year-Olds
by Susan Milord

• • •

Parents' Choice Gold Award
Dr. Toy Best Vacation Product
THE KIDS' NATURE BOOK
365 Indoor/Outdoor Activities and Experiences
by Susan Milord

Williamson's *Tales Alive!*® Books

These beautiful, full-color books focus on retellings of multicultural folktales accompanied by original paintings and activities to round out a child's understanding of a tale and its subject. Books are 96 to 128 pages, full color with original art, 8½ x 11, $12.95 US.

Parents' Choice Honor Award
Skipping Stones Multicultural Honor Award
Benjamin Franklin Best Juvenile Fiction Award
TALES ALIVE!
Ten Multicultural Folktales with Activities
by Susan Milord

• • •

Parents' Choice Approved
Benjamin Franklin Best Juvenile Fiction
Teachers' Choice Award
TALES OF THE SHIMMERING SKY
Ten Global Folktales with Activities
by Susan Milord

• • •

Storytelling World Honor Award
Tales Alive!
BIRD TALES
from Near and Far
by Susan Milord

Williamson's Books

The following **Quick Starts for Kids!**™ books for children, ages 8 and older, are each 64 pages, fully illustrated, trade paper, 8 x 10, $7.95 US.

MAKE YOUR OWN FUN PICTURE FRAMES!
by Matt Phillips

• • •

MAKE YOUR OWN HAIRWEAR!
Beaded Barrettes, Clips, Dangles & Headbands
by Diane Baker

• • •

BAKE THE BEST-EVER COOKIES!
by Sarah A. Williamson

• • •

BE A CLOWN!
Techniques from a Real Clown
by Ron Burgess

• • •

Dr. Toy 100 Best Children's Products
Dr. Toy 10 Best Socially Responsible Products
MAKE YOUR OWN BIRDHOUSES & FEEDERS
by Robyn Haus

• • •

YO-YO!
Tips & Tricks from a Real Pro
by Ron Burgess

• • •

Oppenheim Toy Portfolio Best Book Award
DRAW YOUR OWN CARTOONS!
by Don Mayne

• • •

KIDS' EASY KNITTING PROJECTS
by Peg Blanchette

• • •

KIDS' EASY QUILTING PROJECTS
by Terri Thibault

• • •

American Booksellers Pick of the Lists
MAKE YOUR OWN TEDDY BEARS & BEAR CLOTHES
by Sue Mahren